Foreword by Bestselling Author

TIM MARKS

Conflict Resolution

THE 8 VITAL PRINCIPLES

LIFE Leadership Essentials Series

OBSTACLES
PRESS

First Edition, December 2014
10 9 8 7 6 5 4 3 2 1

Published by:

Obstaclés Press
200 Commonwealth Court
Cary, NC 27511

lifeleadership.com

ISBN 978-0-9909619-2-5

Cover design and layout by Norm Williams, nwa-inc.com

Printed in the United States of America

Peace is not absence of conflict, it is the ability to handle conflict by peaceful means.

—RONALD REAGAN

Contents

FOREWORD
BY TIM MARKS

Since the beginning of time there has been conflict, both big and small. Conflict can range from forgetting to refill the coffee pot to a civil war that tears a country apart. Sadly, the effect of unresolved conflict can cause pain and destruction that rages through history.

We've heard that the only two certainties in life are death and taxes. I would add a third: experiencing conflict. Unless you're a hermit, you're going to interact with other human beings. And at some point, someone is going to step on the other guy's toes. While we can all expect to see conflict, it is very rare to actually witness the successful resolution of conflict.

While most people probably desire conflict resolution, many people are ill-equipped to accomplish it. They either don't have the tools in their communication toolbox, lack the experience to navigate the proverbial minefield without setting off another bomb, or lack the emotional control to handle themselves diplomatically. Sadly, the biggest challenge some people face is the anger they hold in their heart toward the other person.

In some extreme circumstances, the issue at hand might be one of principle. There are times when the situation is black-and-white and there is no room for compromise.

In those moments, we must stand our ground. This is the exception, however. Many circumstances are merely issues of misunderstanding, poor delivery, or sheer conflict avoidance. Most people want conflict to resolve, but some people are selfishly satisfied only if it resolves in their favor.

So where do we turn to learn how to resolve conflict? Some people would say the answers are a Google search away. You'll find life coaches, online seminars, and even entire institutes dedicated to the resolution of conflict. You can read an eBook, watch a YouTube video, or listen to a podcast. Technology is such an amazing thing. Unfortunately, for every benefit that the internet brings, it also brings an equal measure of negativity. Technology creates a physical gap between us and our would-be competitor. Some people would prefer to hide behind technology rather than meet face-to-face. Additionally, with the advent of social media and the explosive increase in text messaging, a comment shared online without the accompanying sound of a diplomatic delivery could be misinterpreted to be much harsher than it was intended. Technology can create massive miscommunication. Many relationships have been damaged because of this, and the offending party never even realized they had hurt the other person's feelings until it was too late.

Conflict Resolution: The 8 Vital Principles will help you prepare yourself for the inevitable conflicts you will face at home and at work. It will help you identify conflict and then teach you a proven step-by-step process to successfully work through it. You can learn and master the principles in this book to resolve conflict, help others feel good about the process and the results, and Lord willing, preserve the vital relationships that make our lives so worthwhile. God Bless.

– Tim Marks, Bestselling author of *Voyage of a Viking and Confidence of a Champion*

Expect Conflict and Be Prepared to Resolve It

Guess what? You have people problems. How do we know? Because you live and work with people. It's really that simple. People can be wonderful, fun, loyal, creative, faithful, and amazing, among many other positive qualities. They also can be unfair, harsh, rude, critical, hurtful, and even abusive. That's just the way it is.

This is true in families, school, the community, business, and every other walk of life. It's even more of a challenge if you're a leader. Why? Because you aren't just working with people when you're the leader in any endeavor; you're also working with people who work with people, who are working with people. More to the point, as a leader you take responsibility for results, and that always involves getting others to perform and work together.

Predictably, human relations bring challenges. There will be conflicts. The best leaders learn how to hit conflict head-on, not only "handling" it but often turning the problem into something productive.

There are some key lessons that all successful leaders eventually learn about conflict resolution. There aren't that many — only about eight. But if you don't know and apply these eight vital principles, human challenges can make your leadership messy and your life a frustrating experience.

On the other hand, if you *do* know these eight key ideas and practice them, you'll have a very different experience. Sadly, few people in the corporate or business world really know these eight principles — the 3 Prerequisites and 5 Steps of truly successful conflict resolution. Those who *do* understand and engage this important wisdom naturally become better leaders. People turn to them for help, and they know what to do in almost any difficult situation.

Stephen Covey taught that principles are important because they are universal, meaning they are nuggets of wisdom that are applicable in pretty much every circumstance. If you learn to master them, even in tough situations, you'll be on the path to top leadership. If not, your success will be obstructed by your own inability to deal with something every leader repeatedly faces — conflict between people. As bestselling author Chris Brady put it, "Problems are the price of success." He also noted, "If you are fighting for something that matters, the obstacles don't."

Business leader Orrin Woodward said: "Becoming skilled at conflict resolution is essential for all good relationships as well as fostering positive long-term connections. In any group of people, the ability to resolve conflict is essential. For example, every successful city has developed processes to handle garbage quickly, efficiently, and effectively. Can you imagine what a city would look like if it didn't handle garbage well?

"In the same way, every leader must have a plan to handle conflict (garbage) in his or her organization. Leaders need to resolve conflict at the source, strengthening relationships through a better understanding of the expectations on both sides of any conflict."

To become highly proficient at this vital skill, it is crucial to learn the 3 Prerequisites and 5 Steps covered in this little book. That's what we're going to learn—the eight fundamental principles of highly effective conflict resolution. These skills aren't hard to develop, if you know what to do. Knowing a few of them will make you a much better leader, and knowing *all* of them will help you genuinely master this truly important skill. As a leader, this is invaluable to your success.

We'll begin by learning how to adopt the right mind-set. Most people try to avoid as much conflict as possible, but when conflict inevitably does occur, such avoidance only causes more problems. In fact, a habit of avoidance almost always turns little issues into major disasters. Top leaders know that conflict is going to happen, so they keep a constant lookout for it. When they see it, they immediately jump in and nip it in the bud before it can become a serious problem. Poor leaders just keep trying to avoid it.

Adopting the right mind-set for great leadership means getting smart about conflict and taking the leadership approach instead of getting caught in the quicksand of avoidance.

It is vital to do these steps in order. Even the most experienced leaders know that skipping a step is always a bad idea. It leaves conflict and deep feelings unresolved, and these always find a way to fester, grow, and then resurface later in negative ways. It's better to address them head on and fully resolve them as soon as possible.

Conflict resolution is an essential leadership skill. In fact, it is important for leaders to become not only capable but actually proficient at resolving conflicts, including those involving the leader himself. The mind-set and steps are the same in all situations where resolution is needed.

In short, highly effective conflict resolution skills are vital for any leader—or anyone who wants to become a leader. Without them, your leadership will stagnate, and your success will be diminished.

PART ONE

Adopt the Right Mind-Set!

Most people do a lot of wrong things when they face conflict. For example, they typically avoid conflict at almost all costs, they frequently nurse their hurts for a long time before they actually talk to the other person, they often talk about a conflict with other people instead of the one who can really fix the problem, and sometimes they gossip or criticize in an attempt to feel better about themselves and the situation.

Then, when they do work up the nerve to talk to the other person in the conflict, many people try to take the easy way out by leaving a message online, on voice mail, or by sending a note. These types of avoidance actually just create more problems.

All these mistakes — and others like them — are the result of the wrong mind-set, and these mistakes can turn small issues or misunderstandings into major problems.

Top leaders avoid these mistakes because they adopt the right mind-set.

Directly and Immediately Address the Appropriate Party Instead of Dwelling on Hurts

If you've been hurt by someone, talk to the person who hurt you. Directly. Don't wait. Do it right away. Of course, don't do it angrily or without following the important principles in this book. Follow these Prerequisites and Steps closely. Exactly, in fact. But don't wait.

One of the best resources on effective conflict resolution is a speech given by Orrin Woodward entitled "Conflict Resolution—Relationships for Life." Since he addressed this important topic so well, we've included a summary of some of his main points in teaching the first two prerequisites. He said: "Conflict is like a fire. Easy to snuff out when it is small, but nearly impossible to handle when not dealt with quickly.

"Imagine going to bed at night and glancing in the corner of your bedroom and seeing a small flame flickering. You decide to ignore it, and you go to bed thinking you'll address it in the morning. This is probably not a good plan, if you like your house. And not addressing conflict immediately and directly isn't a good plan if you'd like to maintain your good relationships and success."

Conflict occurs in every relationship. This is just part of human interaction. "How you maintain key relationships is critical in your ability to lead. Hurt feelings, which lead to conflict, start when one's expectations of another person's commitments and responsibilities are left unfulfilled.

"This can happen for many reasons, including some as innocent as a lack of communication about one's expectations." So the first role of a leader is to help members of the group set the right expectations. This is part of adopting the right mind-set.

Jane Austen wrote, "To wish was to hope, and to hope was to expect." While this is characteristically vague and satirical, it teaches an important point: Everyone has expectations, pretty much all the time. As Austen would say, this is "a truth universally acknowledged." Leaders need to understand this and act accordingly.

To get the right mind-set, begin by clarifying your expectations. If you find yourself in a conflict or helping two people who are in conflict, ask yourself what the expectations were. If you didn't have failed expectations, you wouldn't feel any sense of hurt or conflict. So be specific: what expectations weren't met? Know the answer to this before you move on.

Once you clarify what expectations weren't met, the next part of getting into the right mind-set is to ask yourself why the other person may have failed to meet your expectation. Always *(always!)* ascribe the best intentions to the other person during this brainstorming. Never assume the worst intentions. This approach, this mind-set, is a huge part of being a real leader.

The best leaders don't jump to negatives. They jump to positives. They may find out later that they were wrong, but great leaders don't start by doubting people and ascribing the worst intentions to their actions. They begin by giving others the benefit of the doubt. They think of the best possible explanations and choose to operate with these in mind until they find out the exact truth.

Perhaps the person who hurt you "just didn't understand what the expectations were," Woodward taught. "Sitting down quickly with the other party, lovingly addressing the situation, and apologizing for your role in the mix-up, will do wonders in restoring the bonds of friendship. This will strengthen the speed of trust in your relationships.

"Everyone in the group or community is responsible to convey the mutual expectations in every relationship. Improved communication will nip conflict at its source, reducing issues to deal with, since most people want to perform up to the expectations of others. But even when the expectations are spelled out, there will still be conflicts. We are all human beings, capable of so much good, but also imperfect, impetuous, unreasonable, and overly emotional at times....

"Only a coward will dwell on his disappointments, running them over and over in his mind like a never-ending instant replay—while avoiding the only person able to heal his wounds."

This is powerful. When you encounter a conflict, immediately and lovingly go straight to the other party. Work things out, right away. Have courage, and take action.

"Cowards prefer their hurt feelings to a restored relationship. As the old saying goes, bitterness and resentment are like drinking poison and expecting someone else to die! Don't get bitter, but do get braver! Be brave enough to sit down with the other person and seek to understand why the expectations on both sides are unfulfilled."

Martial artist and actor/director Rati Tsiteladze said, "One will not break through to the enemy with theory. Directness is most important, when in front of the lions' den." This is true whether you are dealing with an actual enemy or with friends and colleagues in times of failed expectations and conflict. Being direct matters!

Make a rule for yourself, as Woodward suggests: "If you think about a hurt more than once (meaning you can't forgive it the first time), you need to address it directly as soon as humanly possible. Not in a spirit of attacking, but in a spirit of understanding. Don't judge or assign motives. Ask! Find out directly!" When you assign negative motives to another person, you are almost always wrong about the motives and the details. Don't wonder. Be brave, and go ask. This is leadership.

"It's hard enough when emotions are high to determine your own motives, let alone omnisciently knowing the motives of others. Stop playing God, and stop trying to read people's minds during conflict. By assuming the best of intentions in the other person, you'll find less bitterness and a real spirit of conciliation. Reflect less on the hurt and more on fellowship with the troubled relationship."

In short, the first response to any hurt or conflict should be to do the following:

- Clarify what expectations weren't met.
- Brainstorm and ascribe the best intentions to the other person.
- Contact the other person directly and talk with him or her.
- Use the 5 Steps below.
- Do this all immediately, without giving any hurt or negativity time to rankle or grow.

This may seem hard, but it is the way real leaders respond to conflict or even potential conflict. They take action. This bears repeating: First, leaders take a few moments to think about what really bothered them—the actual expectation that wasn't fulfilled. Then they ascribe the best intentions to the other person, at least for now. Third, they meet directly with the other person and follow the 5 Steps of great conflict resolution. And they do this all immediately. They don't wait around for hurt feelings to fester. They also do this face to face, whenever possible.

We'll say more on this below, as we learn more about the 5 Steps in detail, but first we need to learn two more very important Prerequisites of highly effective conflict resolution. Through it all, however, this first key remains essential: handle conflicts immediately, by going directly to the other party in the situation.

PREREQUISITE B

Discuss Concerns with the Other Party Instead of Gossiping

Sadly, too often people who feel hurt avoid talking to the other party directly. They talk to a bunch of *other* people instead. This is not only ironic; it is the worst possible choice in tough situations. In order to make their point, most people who do this start saying various negative things about the other party — often long before that person has any idea that a situation is even happening.

This is gossip. It is also criticism. And both of these are the enemies of leadership and success.

In the last section, Prerequisite A, we discussed how important it is not to let hurt and negative feelings *grow* by waiting to address them. In this section, the goal is to make sure that the conflict doesn't *spread* either.

When a hurt person takes his or her negatives to the other people in the group, family, or business — or even to people who have nothing at all to do with the conflict — it causes a lot of unnecessary and absolutely worthless pain. It touches people who have no reason to care but are pulled into a frustrating vortex of negativity. It can hurt reputations and undermine success and progress. And it accomplishes nothing positive. Nothing at all.

A lot of people can get hurt in the process. Don't gossip. Stephen Covey called not gossiping "having integrity to those not present." He was right on. Gossip seldom helps anyone, and it can hurt many.

Orrin Woodward said: "People can take a small misunderstanding and, by violating the principles of good conflict management, use a very small thing to ruin lifetime friendships, simply because the offended party prefers to nurse the hurt rather than nurse the relationship. How sad for both parties, not to mention the community that suffers from the residual damage associated with the immature actions of one, if not both, of the parties."

This is one reason it is so vital to adopt the right mind-set. Go directly and immediately to the other party. Period. Do it lovingly and with understanding. But go. And don't go gossiping or criticizing to other people.

Don't just try to hold it in. When conflict isn't resolved, it doesn't go away but only goes underground. Conflict will be talked about, eventually — if not with the person involved, then with some who are *not* involved. Again, the word for this is *gossip*. And gossip is the sound of cowardice.

Gossip is often used to justify one's position with others, when it has not been justified by legitimate conflict resolution. Sadly, many communities and groups have been destroyed by this cowardly behavior. Woodward taught, "Gossip is one of the most cowardly but also common behaviors known to mankind. It happens when a party is hurt but is unwilling or unable to sit down with the other party to resolve the conflict.

"Because the hurt isn't resolved, one or both parties seek to justify their position through character assassination.... Sadly, this hurts many innocent people who should never be privy to someone's dirty laundry. Only those who are part of the solution should be involved."

Don't gossip. Go directly to the other party, and work things out.

Also, don't help spread or encourage gossip. "If someone gossips to you, ask them, 'Can I quote you on this?' Let the gossiper know that you are taking this information directly to the person gossiped about. This will do two key things: 1) it will let people know you are a person who doesn't feed gossip, and 2) when you go to the harmed party, the one gossiped about, you build his trust by not keeping secrets and by ending the merry-go-round of gossip." This is how great leaders deal with gossip: directly, immediately, firmly, and lovingly.

"Garbage must be cleaned out of a culture, not cultivated. Biblically, character assassinations are just one level removed from an *actual* assassination. Don't play with this fire. Put it out quickly, upholding the reputation of all involved—seeking to put out fires, not fan them."

The same is true of criticism, which is just a type of gossip. "The world is filled with people who, unwilling to improve themselves, choose to tear down others. They think they'll make themselves feel higher by trying to lower others. Refuse to play this game — rather, choose to be like the biggest leaders, who speak all the good they can about others."

Bertrand Russell said, "No one gossips about other people's secret virtues." But they *should!* And despite Russell's view, leaders *do!* As Woodward put it: "The biggest leaders *do* speak behind others' backs, but they speak only the good things. Nothing builds trust like building others up. But when someone comes to you in an attempt to cast aspersions on another person's character, your role shouldn't be to take sides."

"You may not have asked for this role, but when a leader is drawn into the circle of gossip, he chooses to become part of the solution. Tell people: 'Either go back to the person and try to fix things together, or both of us can go to the person and fix it.' These are the only two options, since proper leadership doesn't gossip — but does address and resolve."

To summarize, conflicts *will* happen. People are people, and misunderstandings, hurts, failed expectations, and other conflicts will come. Leaders know this, and they prepare for it. Specifically, when any hurt or conflict comes, they take action by:

1. Clarifying what expectations weren't met.
2. Ascribing the best intentions to the other person.
3. Not allowing worries, hurts or other negatives to fester.
4. Never, ever gossiping about or criticizing the other party.
5. Contacting the other person directly and lovingly resolving things (using the 5 Steps).
6. Doing this all immediately, without giving negative feelings time to grow.

This is the leadership approach, the mature way of responding to conflict.

PREREQUISITE C

Meet Face to Face to Address Conflicts Instead of Relying on Electronic Communications

If you apply the thoughts covered in the last two Prerequisites, your mind-set will be placed to deal effectively with conflict. As you can see by now, the idea is simply to choose the most positive, adult, mature response to hurts and negatives. This is an essential part of leadership.

Even when people adopt the right mind-set, they sometimes make the mistake of communicating conflicts and negatives indirectly. This usually happens with e-mail, on voice messages, or by social media. The problem is that any kind of noninteractive communication tends to fuel the fire of conflict—not quench it.

For example, Mike enjoyed his job speaking for various corporations at their annual or other training events. As his success increased, he hired an agent to book his events and manage his keynoting schedule. His agent, Carol, was efficient and professional, and over several years she helped his business significantly expand.

One day Mike perused his e-mail and saw a note from Carol. He opened it and read:

Mike,

Your speech on September 4 in Atlanta has been bumped. I received an invitation to keynote this event for you and also for Keith Brown, another of my clients. Our policy is always to book the speaker with the biggest honorarium in such situations, but Keith was unavailable on that date so I sent you the request. I just found out that Keith's schedule has changed, and I haven't contacted the company yet to tell them that you're on—so I need to switch this to Keith. Sorry for the confusion. I know this is a bad mix-up, and I feel terrible about it. I hope you'll understand that I had to follow our policy. My boss always demands it. I'm terribly sorry. Please forgive me. I'll try to make it up to you.

Thanks for understanding,

Carol

How would you feel if you were Mike? On the one hand, she came right out and told you what happened. She did it immediately, and she sent you the note directly. Nobody else even knows, so you probably haven't lost any face.

But still, this is a financial setback, and at the very least a bit frustrating.

But it's worse than that. Carol made a number of mistakes simply by e-mailing this note. First of all, little words like *bumped* and *bigger honorarium* are hurtful in this format. Clearly Carol didn't mean to offend her client. She was actually attempting to do just the opposite.

If Mike rereads this e-mail over and over, however, as many people would, he's likely to fixate on *bumped* and *bigger honorarium* and begin to think that maybe Carol is sending him a hidden message. "Does she really want to work with me? Is she truly representing me the way I want her to when she deals with clients?" And so on. Eventually he'll probably arrive here: "She must want to dump me as a client. At the very least, she just sees me as 'another client.' Those are the words she used. What's up with her?"

This can cause feelings of concern, frustration, confusion, and possibly hurt.

The second major problem with Carol's format is that it's almost impossible for Mike to really *feel* the depth of her apology. After all, he can't even hear her voice. He can't see her face or read her body language. He can't tell if she means it, or how much she means it. A short written note is a very *cold* way to hear something negative. All the emphasis is naturally on the *negative* words, and the words of apology don't feel strong at all. In fact, they are so short and unfeeling that Mike may get offended. Even if he chooses a mature response, he'll probably have moments where he has to fight off the temptation to take offense.

A third major mistake is that Carol's note was noninteractive. Mike can't just ask her questions, try to clarify what she means at any point, or express his frustration. And she has no chance to immediately resolve his concerns, because in an e-mail she simply won't know what they are—or even that he has them.

In addition, the very fact that she chose to do this in an e-mail message where Mike is not allowed to interact or ask questions also feels cold. It's as if she's admitting that this will be tough for Mike, but she chose this means of communication intentionally so Mike would just have to "deal with it." What is communicated is that she doesn't care enough to give Mike a chance to meaningfully interact.

Because he can't interact directly, he may automatically do the worst thing he can: play the "conversation" over and over in his mind, expressing his frustrations and imagining the negative things she'll say in response. The longer he does this, the more things escalate and the worse their relationship is going to get. Of course, the saddest part is that he's making it all up!

If she had called him or met with him in person, he could tell her real thoughts, ask real questions, listen to her actual responses, and quickly understand where they stand. So could she, for that matter. Carol could hear his responses and know when things are resolved, versus when to keep apologizing—or even offering some kind of remedy or compensation.

But in a written note, neither of them have these options. Mike is left to his own imagination, and since the message contained negative news to begin with, his imaginings probably won't do either of them much good.

Now imagine that Mike decides to respond the same way, by e-mail. Or by voice mail. Big mistake. He can do it immediately and directly to Carol, but using a noninteractive medium to address his hurt or dashed expectations is a very bad idea. Just consider:

Carol,

This is very bad news. I really feel upset by it. You should have worked out the scheduling before notifying me, or you should honor your word once you've informed me of the event.

Mike

Pretty straightforward. But how will it make Carol feel, and how will she react? She'll likely start imagining and playing conversations in her head, and the whole thing will get worse. After all, he basically just told her she lacks integrity. He might as well have sent her a Flash Graphic with the words "Liar, Liar, Pants on Fire!" flashing and surrounded by flames.

In truth, his expectations have been dashed, and right now he's probably feeling that she needs more integrity. "She's my *agent*, after all!" he keeps telling himself. At the same time, she's tempted to think that he's just a diva. "After *all* I've done for him. How ungrateful!"

Even if these two professionals control their thoughts and avoid such negative (and immature) thinking, they'll still be tempted by these kinds of thoughts. Why not avoid the temptation and possibility of hurt and just talk directly—as soon as possible? Why not go straight to the source and work things out?

Amazingly, a lot of people avoid this obvious solution. Leaders must rise above this natural human tendency of avoidance.

The bottom line is that this noninteractive format has both parties working from behind. Neither really knows what the other person is thinking or feeling, and neither can be sure of the other person's intentions. They need to speak directly.

Fortunately, in this situation, Mike restrained himself because he wanted to really think about the e-mail before sending it. He showed the e-mail to his wife, who is also his business partner, and she suggested that he simply give Carol a call. "She's been so professional, this just doesn't add up. You need to just ask her what's up. Be kind, and remember all she's done for you. Also, don't assume you know what her intentions are. She didn't mean anything negative by 'bumped' or 'bigger honorarium.' She was probably just busy, worried about your reaction, and hoping her apology would be enough. Just call her, Mike."

Mike immediately relaxed, and then he got on the phone and called Carol. No e-mail response. Just a call. She was unavailable, so he left a message: "Carol, hi. Please give me a call. Thanks! I'm excited to hear from you."

"Well done," his wife said.

Later, when Carol called, Mike didn't rehash the e-mail or try to point out its flaws or her need to honor her commitment. He simply said, "Oh, hello, Carol. Thanks for calling. I got your e-mail. Can you tell me about the Atlanta event?"

As they discussed the situation, Mike could tell that Carol was really upset about the situation. She didn't say so, but he got the sense that her new boss was making things difficult for her. He asked several questions, and finally he said, "Carol, let me ask you a question. This is really strange for me, because our interaction has always been so professional, and I was really counting on this event. I won't pretend I'm not frustrated, because I am. But what if we just put it behind us and move on?

"Specifically, can you do me a favor? Would you try to think of a way to make it even *better* for both of us? I was expecting the honorarium for this, maybe you can help us get another, new event that will take its place. That way, we can both move on to bigger and better things. What do you think?"

There was a pause on the line, then Carol said, "Actually, I have an idea. Can I get back with you?"

Four days later Mike signed a new contract for a three-speech tour to a company's US, Canadian, and Mexican headquarters. Each speech paid the same honorarium as the one single event in Atlanta—for a total of three times the original. "I told my boss we owed you one," Carol told him, "and he agreed. I think you'll be a real hit with this organization."

Sometimes the right communication can make all the difference. Most of the time, in fact. Moreover, the wrong communication is worse than a bad solution—it usually causes additional problems.

In a nutshell, whenever you have anything negative to communicate, especially dealing with any kind of conflict or potential conflict, do it face to face if possible and at the very least in person on the phone (or using one of the many video-chat options available today). Never try to resolve conflict using a noninteractive format. If you have to send an e-mail or leave a message, just be positive and tell the person you'd love to talk to them and look forward to their call. Then deal directly with them in person.

The bigger the real or potential negative, hurt, or conflict, the closer you need to be as you work together for a great solution. If the conflict is deep or highly emotional, do it in person. Never try to engage in conflict resolution through e-mail, social media, or voice mail.

SUMMARY

Adopt the Right Mind-Set

Conflicts will come,
and leaders don't avoid them.

When a problem arises,
deal with it directly.

Deal with it immediately.

Know specifically what expectations
weren't met.

Always ascribe the best motivations
to the other party, unless they personally
tell you otherwise.

Don't allow hurts or conflicts
to fester or grow.

Don't spread the problem to other people:
never gossip or criticize behind
someone's back.

Protect the other party's reputation.

Don't communicate negatives
or potential negatives in any noninteractive
format — talk in person.

The bigger the problem, the more you
need to be physically closer when
you resolve things.

PART TWO

The 5 Steps of Effective Conflict Resolution

Now that you're adopting the right mind-set, it's time to learn the 5 Steps. Whenever a conflict arises between you and someone else, or between people you lead, take action.

Remember to do it immediately, don't wait around, don't let things fester, never gossip, and do things face to face or at least on the phone rather than leaving any kind of noninteractive message.

And when you meet, follow the 5 Steps!

STEP 1

Affirm the Relationship

With the right mind-set in place, the steps of highly-effective conflict resolution are simple and straightforward. Step 1 is to Affirm the Relationship. Sit down with the other party, and tell them: "I may be uncomfortable, but I am here because I value our relationship much more than my comfort and more than the details of the conflict."

Communicate that "I'm sure there was some misunderstanding, and I want to know how I could have done better and in turn, make it right."

Do this in a spirit of caring, love, and honest desire to bridge any gaps.

There. That's Step 1.

It is incredibly important to do this at the beginning of any conflict resolution. If you try to skip this step, the whole resolution will probably fail. It's that essential and that powerful.

Bruce's Example

Bruce was the leader of a successful business, and over the years he increasingly learned how to effectively work with people. He became skilled at using the 5 Steps of effective conflict resolution, and he knew that this was a big part of his success. Without it, his relationships simply couldn't have supported the growth of his organization.

One summer his older daughter Carmen and her husband and young children visited for a ten-day vacation. They had a wonderful time barbecuing in the back yard, watching the fireworks on the holiday, and talking late into the evenings after the kids were down for the night. It was a special time of bonding and reconnecting with loved ones.

One incident had the potential to hurt Bruce's relationship with Carmen. It started when Bruce noticed that Carmen was a very kind and attentive mother to her children, but sometimes took a negative tone toward her nine-year-old sister Melanie, his youngest daughter.

The first time it happened, Bruce ascribed it to normal tension because everyone was trying to hurry before an event. But as the behavior persisted, he began to grow concerned. When Melanie started staying in her room instead of participating in fun family time together, he realized that the situation needed a remedy. But what should he do? After all, Carmen was an adult now and didn't need to be "bossed by Daddy."

Bruce prayerfully considered the situation, counseled with his wife, and decided that something should be done.

He simply couldn't stand by and watch little Melanie wilt and feel hurt. Even though he knew that the two daughters loved each other very much and that Carmen wasn't in any way intentionally trying to hurt her sister. In fact, most of the time he saw that Carmen was a great friend to Melanie and that the younger girl craved and loved her older sister's positive attention.

But the few times Carmen snapped at Melanie or expressed anger were hurting the relationship and the family dynamic. It didn't look like something that would just go away, and Bruce knew from years of leadership that taking action early, directly, and lovingly could really help.

That evening he asked Carmen if he could meet with her, and once they were alone she asked, "What did you want to talk about?"

It was at this point that Bruce made a mistake. He had all the right intentions, he spoke in a loving and happy tone of voice, and he had addressed his concern both directly and in a timely fashion. But, momentarily forgetting all his years of leadership experience and the fact that the first Step of conflict resolution is to Affirm the Relationship, he just jumped straight into the problem.

He said, "Carmen, I want you to stop being so mean to Melanie."

Carmen stiffened a tiny bit, surprised at what she perceived as a direct attack from her usually loving and supportive father. She immediately began to think of reasons that Melanie had deserved a tough response. She started looping in her mind about various ways she had been very nice to Melanie and how Dad's words were simply untrue. And the prideful part of her whispered in her mind about how she was an adult now and didn't need a lecture or scolding.

"I'm not *so* mean to her," she said. "I've snapped at her a few times when she needed it, but I've spent the whole week being nice to her and going out of my way to help her…"

Bruce was taken aback by this response, so he outlined the three specific occasions he had witnessed, pointing out Carmen's flawed behaviors in each instance and suggesting what she should have done in each case. With every word, Carmen felt more and more attacked. She felt herself coming close to tears, and this upset her even further. She tried to take control of her emotions by pushing back against her Dad's words.

Five minutes later they were both strongly arguing for their divergent points of view. They were both convinced their own view was right and that the other person's perspective was wrong. They both maintained a civil exterior, but they became increasingly upset on the inside.

Finally Bruce stood and said, "Well, maybe we should talk about this later when we've both had time to calm down and think about it."

Carmen replied, "Please don't just walk away; that's a passive-aggressive response. Let's work this out like adults."

Not wanting to be labeled passive-aggressive, Bruce sat back down, and they kept talking, but each grew increasingly frustrated with the other. The conversation was on the verge of degenerating into real anger when Carmen's husband knocked on the door with a crying two-year-old who had fallen. The toddler wasn't hurt, but he wanted Mommy and wouldn't be consoled by anyone else.

As Bruce and Carmen both turned their full attention to helping comfort the little guy, Bruce suddenly found that he was flooded with feelings of love for his daughter. As the negatives were replaced by this strong sense of care and parental pride for his adult daughter and the way she was living her life, his mind cleared, and he realized his mistake.

He had failed to start the discussion by Affirming the Relationship. *You would never do this with one of your partners, colleagues, or clients*, he told himself silently. *You know better!* He realized that he should have started the conversation with real positives, built up the relationship and mutual confidence, and then introduced his concern without such accusing words.

In fact, it dawned on him that his overwhelming love for his daughter had made him think that he could just skip this step — when the truth is that the closer the relationship, the bigger the chance of real hurt. *I should have been especially good at following the steps in such an important relationship, not more lax about it*, he told himself. *I didn't build a real foundation for this conversation. I assumed it was just there already, because of our family love, but that is never the right way to deal with conflict.*

When the toddler was down for the night, and Carmen returned for the talk, Bruce took an entirely different approach. He apologized for his words and attitude and told Carmen how much he loved her. Then he said, "Can I share with you the thoughts and feelings I've been experiencing this whole week about you? I've been so excited and impressed with what kind of wife, mother, leader, and person you are now. I just can't tell you how impressed I've been."

She looked at him in surprise, and this time a few tears did start to come.

"This thing with Melanie is just a tiny blip, and I probably should have just let it go. It's been one minute out of a whole week, and the whole week I've been so thrilled at how wonderful you are. I can't believe I led with this tiny little thing when your whole visit has been a tidal wave of feelings about how awesome you are. It was stupid of me."

Bruce said nothing else about Melanie but went on, "For example…" Then he shared *specific* instances and details where Carmen had done something that deeply impressed him.

After the fifth example, she finally interrupted him with a laugh… "Okay, Dad, I get it. Wow! I had no idea you were feeling this way. You don't have to keep praising me, I get it. I'll be nicer to Melanie, I promise. I'll go out of my way to fix any rift with her and make her feel loved."

"Oh," he replied. "Okay, that's great. But can I tell you just two more things you did this week that are so amazing?" Without waiting for her response, he launched into his passionate examples.

Twenty minutes later, still laughing, Carmen left his office and went to the kitchen to be with the rest of the adults. Bruce sat back, smiled widely and happily, and turned off his laptop for the night. He headed back into the kitchen to join the family.

Before he turned out the lights and left the office, he stopped at the door and made a mental note: *Always, always, always do* all *the steps. Never skip Step 1. Affirming the Relationship is vital, no matter how close the relationship and no matter how much you might think it's just not necessary in a given occasion. It is always necessary.*

He quickly walked over to his notebook where he kept important thoughts and wrote this down. Then he shut his book, smiled, and walked into the kitchen.

Applications

Step 1 of truly effective conflict resolution is not optional. Leaders who try to skip it quickly learn that, in fact, it is the most important part of effective conflict resolution. The truth is, *every* step is the most important — when it is time for that step. But because Step 1 comes first, and because it is often the most emotionally-charged step, it is absolutely vital.

And as Bruce's story illustrates, it is just as important in family, friendship, and personal relationships as it is in a work setting.

Imagine how much more successful Bruce could have been, at least at the beginning of the conversation, if he had started by saying, "Carmen, I have loved this week! I am really impressed with you and excited about the kind of wife, mother, leader and person you have become. For example...."

After telling her an example or two, he could have said. "I want to do two things in this talk with you. First, I want to ask for your help with Melanie, because I think there is something you can do for her that neither your mother nor I can do as effectively as you. And second, I want to tell you more of the things about you that are impressive to me right now in your life. Can we do these two things?"

"Of course we can."

"Great. About Melanie. I think she really wants to make a positive impression with you, and I'm not sure you realize just how much she hangs on your every word. I noticed when you snapped at her that it really seemed to deflate her, and I wasn't sure if you noticed. I think your relationship is incredibly important to her, and I'm hoping you can really help her. She gives so much emotional weight to anything you say to her, positive or negative.

"To tell the truth, I am a bit uncomfortable bringing this up to you, because, like I said, I've spent this whole week being so impressed with you, and I wouldn't want this small thing to be a negative at all. But I value our relationship much more than my comfort, and your relationship with Melanie can help her a lot—so I hope it's okay if I ask for your help on this."

What a different tone! Step 1 is incredibly powerful. Even if you *could* skip it in a certain circumstance—which no leader can or should—why would anyone ever want to? Step 1 holds so much emotional power that it should always be used to strengthen the relationship.

Again, emphatically: always begin by Affirming the Relationship. This is the only place to start, and without it the rest of the steps will likely never quite come about. In fact, in some cases, just Affirming the Relationship solves the whole problem. This isn't the norm, but it does happen.

When you know that the other person truly, deeply, admires you, respects you, loves you, would do practically anything for you, and is willing and downright excited to do whatever is needed to make things right, it's hard to feel anything negative. When both parties experience such feelings, the conflict is pretty much over.

The other 4 Steps of successful conflict resolution make sure this positivity lasts, but without these affirming positives, resolution is nearly impossible. Step 1 is profoundly effective.

Push the Repeat Button

If there is a conflict or a potential conflict, start in the right place. Affirm the Relationship. Do this at the beginning, and repeat it throughout the other steps. It's almost impossible to overdo this Step. Any time a negative feeling or tone starts to arise, affirm the other person.

Of course, such affirming words must always be genuine and authentic. It simply doesn't work to flatter or make up positives. Be honest, and be open and affirming. The more, the better. Repeat this any time you sense that a positive is needed.

Most people loop negatives in their mind a number of times, so repetitive affirming of positives is necessary to counteract these monkey-mind thoughts. Affirm the Relationship early, and Affirm the Relationship often!

The Emotional Bank Account

An important part of Affirming the Relationship, as Stephen Covey taught, are honest and specific words of praise. People generally have a running "emotional bank account" with any relationship, Covey said, and all negative words or criticisms are withdrawals, while positive words and genuine praise are deposits. Thus, when a conflict arises, it is very important to use the right kind of praise (authentic!) to make deposits in the "emotional bank account" before trying to discuss remedies.

If the other party feels a large deficit in the emotional bank account of his relationship with you, he'll subconsciously resist reconciliation — even if consciously he wants to resolve things. Put in big emotional deposits right from the beginning of your conversation to help balance the account. This is very important.

In short, Affirming the Relationship is Step 1 for a reason. Without it the other person's emotional bank account will be struggling with emotional debt and feelings of fear, frustration, and even mistrust. Genuine, honest praise and expressions of respect, admiration, and love make all the difference. Without them, little progress can be expected. With them, in contrast, miracles can and frequently do happen.

Special Note: Third-Party Leader

Sometimes conflict resolution is best obtained with a mediator or a third-party leader who walks the two "opposing" parties through the 5 Steps. If you are the leader in such a setting, it is important to apply all the same recommendations outlined in this book. When the hurt is deep or has turned to a fight between growing "enemies," the Steps are just as powerful.

As a leader, you'll find it essential to follow them closely and in order. Skipping steps usually dooms the conflict resolution. As you study and learn these steps for yourself, think of how you would apply them as a leader helping two parties try to resolve a conflict. The principles don't change, but the details are slightly different.

For example, in most cases a third-party leader helping two people try to resolve a conflict doesn't have the benefit of making sure Prerequisites A, B, and C have been followed. They probably haven't, in such a situation. Problems and feelings have likely already festered, and actions have probably escalated to intentional attacks by the time the third-party leader gets involved.

With that said, it is still the 5 Steps that will bring about resolution—if one is possible. The leader must deeply know the 5 Steps and help the two parties learn each of them and apply them. If the 5 Steps aren't applied, real resolution probably won't occur. But leaders can have huge influence if the two parties genuinely want a resolution. Asking the two parties to read this book before you meet, or at least verbally teaching both parties each Step as it comes can be extremely helpful.

Again, as you are reading this book, learn how to resolve a conflict when you are one of the parties—but also think about how you would implement each step as a leader working with two other parties in conflict. Keeping this in mind as you read will help you learn two vital leadership skills from this book: (1) how to resolve your conflicts with others (which will inevitably come), and (2) how to apply the 5 Steps as a leader when you are inevitably called upon to help others resolve their conflicts. Great leaders become effective at both.

SUMMARY

Step 1

Start any conversation about resolving
conflict by Affirming the Relationship.

Communicate respect, admiration,
and love for the other person.

Make sure the other knows how much you
care and how enthusiastic you are to
do whatever you can to make
things right.

Use authentic praise.

Be specific in your praise.

Be genuine and honest.

Repeat affirming words
any time a negative arises.

Affirm the Relationship

early and often.

Learn to apply Step 1 (and all 5 Steps)
both in conflicts where you are a party
and also as a leader helping other
people resolve a conflict.

STEP 2

Genuinely Seek to Understand

Once you have Affirmed the Relationship to the point that the other person's emotional bank account feels fuller and he is ready to get down to business, the next step is to Seek to Understand. Don't start by making sure the other party understands you; first focus on understanding the other party.

What were the expectations that weren't met for her? What actually happened that led to this misunderstanding? (Often what you thought happened and what really occurred are not exactly the same.) What were her intentions? What was she thinking? What has she been thinking since?

These are important things to understand, and they usually shed light on what has really occurred. This can clear up a lot of misunderstandings.

But it is important not to simply pepper the other person with these direct questions. Instead, let her explain them in her way, in her own words. Listen intently. Most people aren't very good at this, but leaders must make it a top skill. Really listen.

Stephen Covey taught this principle very effectively: Seek *first* to understand the other person's thoughts and feelings. The way to do this is simple, but not everyone understands it. Even many people who have read how this works forget what to do when true listening is needed.

The Mirror Technique

The key to quality listening is the Mirror Effect, which gives us the Mirror Technique. This means reflecting back what the other person says to you. This is very easy, if only you make a point of doing it. Top leaders learn that this is a must. If you don't do this, you won't usually experience truly effective conflict resolution.

Here are some examples—both good and bad—of mirror listening:

DIALOGUE #1

Connor:

"Okay, thank you for saying that. It makes me feel a lot better. It's been so frustrating knowing you were upset with me but not understanding why. I kept telling myself I didn't do anything wrong, and I guess that made me prideful, and I kept blaming you. I shouldn't have done that."

Mark:

"Connor, I blew this, like I said before. I don't blame you for feeling frustrated. Who wouldn't? It was my fault.

"So, you thought I was going around telling people that you had promised me to come speak for my group in August, and that then I just changed my mind and cancelled without even giving you an explanation?"

Analysis:

NOT EFFECTIVE. At this point, Connor is thinking, "I don't really want to answer his pointed questions. It's like an Inquisition. I wanted to explain myself, not be interrogated." Mark starts well, but then instead of mirroring Connor's words, he goes in a different direction. Let's try it again...

DIALOGUE #2

Connor:

"Okay, thank you for saying that. It makes me feel a lot better. It's been so frustrating knowing you were upset with me but not understanding why. I kept telling myself I didn't do anything wrong, and I guess that made me prideful, and I kept blaming you. I shouldn't have done that."

Mark:

"Connor, I blew this, like I said before. I don't blame you for feeling frustrated. Who wouldn't? It was my fault.

"I just kept feeling that I hadn't promised you I would come in August. We talked about the possibility but never firmed anything up. And then all of a sudden I was hearing that I had lied to you and that I'm not the kind of person who keeps his promises. It hurt, and I got upset."

Analysis:

NOT EFFECTIVE. This is even worse than the interrogational questions in Attempt #1 above. At least with the questions, Connor was allowed to keep talking. In example 2, however, Mark just takes over and focuses on himself. He's trying to be understood first, not seeking first to understand. This can undo all the progress Mark made with Step 1 in Affirming the Relationship, because his refusal to really listen and his use of accusatory words will naturally make Connor wonder if the earlier words of reconciliation were sincere. *Why won't he let me explain myself?* Connor is thinking. Mark needs to really listen, meaning that he needs to use the Mirror Technique. Let's consider another example.

DIALOGUE #3

Connor:

"Okay, thank you for saying that. It makes me feel a lot better. It's been so frustrating knowing you were upset with me but not understanding why. I kept telling myself I didn't do anything wrong, and I guess that made me prideful, and I kept blaming you. I shouldn't have done that."

Mark:

"Connor, I blew this, like I said before. I don't blame you for feeling frustrated. Who wouldn't? It was my fault.

"So you weren't sure why I was upset, and you felt that you hadn't done anything wrong?"

Analysis:

EFFECTIVE. This is Mirroring. Mark simply repeats back the main points of what Connor said. This affirms that he was really listening, and it invites Connor to elaborate. Connor will naturally feel validated, because Mark clearly repeated the main things Connor just said.

Connor will feel heard, and he'll be ready to discuss more about where he was coming from. If you are seeking to understand, this is how you want the other person to feel, over and over: heard, affirmed, valued. And you want the other person to know that you're ready to hear more. Just repeat the main points of his words back to him.

DIALOGUE #4

Connor:

"Exactly. I kept thinking that it was you who broke our agreement, not me, so why should you be upset? But of course, the truth is that you and I never actually nailed down a date and time. I just kept thinking you would call to set the date. I was hesitant to call you, because I know you are so busy.

"I should have called you, I know. But I was shy about it, and I kept telling myself you would call when you were ready. On the other hand, I was so excited about your second visit to my group that I kept telling people about it. I wanted them to be as excited as you."

Mark:

"That makes sense. We talked about me possibly coming, and you expected me to call you and set a time. In the meantime, you were pumped up about my visit and told people I was coming again. Am I getting it right?"

Analysis:

EFFECTIVE. Mark is simply listening closely, then *showing* Connor that he is listening carefully by mirroring back the main points of what Connor tells him. This affirms Connor, he knows he is heard, and he feels invited to share more.

Keep mirroring until the other person tells you he is finished and has nothing more to say. This may seem like it takes a while, but it is much faster than not listening and forcing Connor to keep his feelings in and letting them fester.

Oh, and note how Mark doesn't argue with Connor or interrupt to clarify. He probably really wants to say, "Wait. I thought *you* were going to call. That's how it should have been — after all, it's *your* event." But he doesn't. He really listens.

If he had interrupted and said this, Connor would have felt, "He's not listening anymore. He just doesn't understand how I feel about this. I wish he'd listen. He said he was going to listen. Now he just wants me to listen to him." That's not effective.

Fortunately, Mark understands Step 2 of effective conflict resolution, and he's truly listening. How do we know? Because he's mirroring everything

Connor says, and you can only effectively mirror if you are genuinely listening.]

DIALOGUE #5

Connor:

"Yes, you are getting it. That's exactly how I felt. I kept thinking that I needed to call you, and then I kept feeling that calling would be too forward, and I needed to just let you call me on your own schedule. And I never openly announced that you were coming.

"I told my closest partner, because I was so excited, and I made him promise to keep it a secret. Then I told another member of my group, because he was struggling, and I thought it would help him get excited. I told him to keep it a secret too.

"As the weeks passed, I told several people, and then when two months had passed I had to tell them I thought you weren't coming in August, and I felt bad. I don't know who started saying that you had broken your promise—it sure wasn't me. But I can see that I caused the whole problem by not calling you and by telling people I thought you'd be coming even though we hadn't set the details. I shouldn't have done that."

Mark:

"You know what, Connor. I think you're great, and you were just trying to motivate people, right? At first you thought we were planning on August, and when I never called, you weren't sure what to do. And other people started feeling like I'd flaked on you, and you didn't know what to do, right?"

Connor:

"Yes. That's exactly right. I know I should have called you directly at that point, but by then I just didn't know why you hadn't called, and I felt so much pressure from all the people who were expecting you. Of course, that was my fault too. I should have told them all directly that you hadn't bailed on us at all, because we hadn't set an exact time. But by then I heard that you were upset with me and I...I guess I just wasn't thinking clearly. I should have just called. I really blew it."

Mark:

"So by the time you realized you could have called me to clarify, you heard that I was frustrated, and you didn't know what to do. That makes sense. Am I understanding you correctly?"

Analysis:

EFFECTIVE. Mark is mirroring whatever Connor says, over and over. He is also putting a positive spin on it, giving Connor the benefit of the doubt on everything. Connor can't help but feel affirmed and heard. That's Step 1 (affirmed) and Step 2 (heard) in a nutshell. In fact, by this point, Connor is breathing a deep sigh of relief. *He's heard me, and he understands me.*

This accomplishes two vitally important things. First, it puts Connor in a place where he feels really heard. This naturally prepares him to actually hear the other person's viewpoint. Without this, conflict resolution is impossible.

Second, now that Connor is feeling heard, his own emotional bank account feels full, and he can start to breathe and relax a little. When this happens, his mind is going to automatically start telling him what he did wrong. This is much more effective coming from Connor's own mind than from anything Mark, or anybody else, says.

Until Connor feels heard, he won't feel understood. And until he feels understood, he will be so focused on his own viewpoint that he can't really settle down and grasp how much he blew it. But as soon as he feels genuinely heard (and nothing assures this better than the Mirror Technique), he'll start to feel understood. And when he feels understood, he'll relax his defensive posture, and his mind will start pointing out the flaws in his own behavior.

In fact, right now in the conversation, Connor's brain is probably starting to tell him: *Man, I blew it! I could have called Mark at any point! I shouldn't have told anyone that he was coming in August without actually setting a date with Mark, and once people were blaming him, I should have immediately clarified to everyone that this was my fault. And I should have called Mark to assure him that I blew it and that the whole thing was on me. Oh my gosh! He must think I'm a total idiot. Because I am! I totally messed this up! Will he forgive me?*

If these words come from Mark, they could easily ruin the whole conflict resolution. But if they come from Connor's own brain, he is ready and enthusiastic to do anything he can to resolve the situation. It all hinges on him *first* feeling heard and then feeling understood.

This is the power of seeking first to understand. By mirroring the other person's words, you show him that you are truly listening, and as you keep mirroring him, he'll eventually feel fully understood. At that point, he'll become more objective, and his own brain will do most of the work of making your case for you. If he isn't doing this yet, keep mirroring.

DIALOGUE #6

Connor:

"Yes. Mark, I am so sorry for this. I really blew it. I feel so ridiculous right now. All I had to do was call you. Can you forgive me?"

Mark:

"Of course. You feel terrible about it all, and so do I. Will you forgive me too? I blew it even worse. When I heard that you were saying negative things about me, I knew I should just call you directly. I knew things must not be the way I was hearing. But stupidly, I got my feelings hurt and didn't call. Man, I blew it. Is that how you felt too?"

Mirroring is incredibly powerful. It shows the other person that you are truly listening, and it also shows *you* that you are listening. If you're not mirroring, your mind is probably racing around doing other things—like preparing how to respond or analyzing the other person's ideas for flaws or figuring out what you want for lunch. These are all bad listening techniques.

Mirroring = Listening

Mirroring keeps you focused on what the other person is really saying, and on the other person's needs, wants, and emotional state. When you aren't mirroring the other person's words, you're not really listening. And if you're not listening, the person isn't feeling heard, and you aren't resolving anything. You might actually be adding to the conflict and negatives by not listening.

Use mirroring to really understand the other person's perspective. Really! "By letting the other party unburden himself," Orrin Woodward said, "taking his words not personally but professionally, you allow him to release his hurt feelings. Only after listening, asking mirroring questions to positively clarify and understand, not defending yourself but only to clearly state the other person's position, expressing concern over the pain caused by the conflict, is one ready to move on to the next step.

"Even if you didn't mean to give hurt, you should empathetically accept that hurt was given and seek to make it right. Hurt is caused by unmet expectations," as we said above, "by one or both parties. Understand the expectations, and deeply care about them, even if you never intended any harm."

And always give the other person the benefit of the doubt that he didn't intend any harm either. "State back the other person's views, with the same emotional emphasis on things as he did. Do this over and over, and ask, 'Did I get it right? Do you feel that I really understood you?'"

If the answer is "No" or "Not yet" or even "You're getting closer," it is important to listen more. Repeat this process until the answer is a firm 'Yes! You really understand me now.'

"Genuinely listening to another person is one of the most affirming things you can do to heal hurts, release misunderstandings and even mistakes, and build people." Importantly, all this active listening also shows how much you *care*, and caring is a big part of repairing.

Broad Resolution

This is an interesting list of things that true listening and the Mirror Technique can accomplish. Indeed, this is a vital list of skills for any leader:

- Heal hurts
- Release misunderstandings
- Release mistakes
- Build people

While the focus of this chapter has been on the first three (heal hurts, release misunderstandings, and release mistakes), Step 2 is also incredibly helpful in building people. Even when you aren't resolving a concern, mirroring the other person in a conversation is an invaluable leadership skill. Use it to build people, in many settings.

Top leaders are excellent listeners, usually because they have developed this skill, and *great* leaders are truly *great* listeners. You can't be a great leader without learning to be a great listener and turning this ability into a habit and a strength. The key to great listening and to Step 2 is mirroring.

Just like Step 1, don't ever skip Step 2. It is easy to forget in a heated moment when emotions are high, but this will always decrease the effectiveness of your conflict resolution and may keep it from happening at all. Effective leaders know that to resolve conflict, it is essential to explicitly follow Step 1 and then Step 2. There are no substitutes for these crucial Steps in fixing a relationship that is struggling or broken. Listening is incredibly healing.

People need to feel heard, and when they do, they can feel understood. Only at this point can they be emotionally ready to think in terms of real solutions. If you actually want to resolve a conflict, you simply must seek first to truly understand. Listen intently, using the Mirror Technique over and over until the other person tells you that you have fully understood him.

SUMMARY

Step 2

Seek First to Understand by mirroring.

Learn and practice
the Mirror Technique.

Keep mirroring (real listening) until
the other person assures you
he feels fully heard and
truly understood.

Don't stop mirroring to ask questions that
take the person on a tangent.

Don't stop mirroring to clarify or justify your
perspective on things the person says.

Don't interrupt mirroring to point out
flaws, mistakes, or factual errors
in the person's account.

In short, don't stop mirroring

until the person firmly believes
he has been well heard
and really understood.

You can tell the Mirror Technique
is working when the person begins
pointing out how he is responsible
for parts of the situation.

Until this happens, he has more
to say.

Mirroring can be used to build
people in many ways — not just
in conflict resolution. It is the key
to quality listening.

Become skilled at mirroring
by practicing it often in
many settings.

Always remember that it is
people who feel hurt who hurt people.
To heal, such people need
to feel understood.

To feel understood, people
need to feel heard.

Mirroring nearly always makes
people feel heard.

STEP 3

Lovingly Seek to Be Understood

Once Steps 1 and 2 are complete, and not before, share the issues lovingly from your perspective. The key word here is *lovingly!* If you don't come across as loving, your explanations will usually fall on deaf ears. How your communications *feel* are often more important than the actual words you use.

Be sure both the words and the feelings are truly loving. If not, you can undo much of what you've accomplished in Steps 1 and 2.

Lean Loving

Chris Brady taught that most people naturally lean either in the direction of love or courage. In leadership, these often translate as either "loving" or "reprimanding." Know which one is your natural tendency, and use this knowledge in dealing with people.

If you tend toward reprimanding, for example, you'll usually need to go out of your way to be sure you seem loving to other people. Just *intending* to be loving isn't enough. The other party must actually *feel* that you are being loving.

And even if you usually tend toward loving, don't just assume that the other person will feel your love. Make sure. Hopefully, because you genuinely and effectively sought to understand during Step 2 using the Mirror Technique, he will now listen intently and openly to you. Even if he doesn't, you can at least say enough to get your point across.

Note that many people naturally lean toward loving in some roles in their life and at the same time lean to reprimanding in other roles. If you lean toward loving at work but more typically lean in the direction of reprimanding with your kids, for example, take this into account. If you are resolving a concern with one of your children, you'll have to work harder to really communicate a loving demeanor than you probably would at work. Again, tailor this to your personal traits and roles.

Do Share and Resolve; Don't Justify, Blame, or Lecture

Again, most of the work of filling the other person's emotional bank account should have been done in Step 2. You don't want to ruin this by taking emotional withdrawals during Step 3. Specifically, as you lovingly share your thoughts and feelings about the situation, remember that resolution is the objective, not justification or any kind of recrimination.

The key is to talk about how you felt, not about what the other party should have done. For example:

DIALOGUE #7

Mark:

"Connor, thank you so much for sharing your thoughts and feelings. I really appreciate knowing what you went through. Before I share my experience, have you said everything you need to say? And have I truly understood you?

"If not, I'm happy to keep listening. I want to make sure I fully understand your perspective on this. Do you feel that I really understood you?"

Connor:

"Yes, I do. Thank you for taking the time to really hear me out. I feel totally understood. I just hope you can forgive me for being so stupid!"

Mark:

"Of course I can, and do. And I hope you'll forgive me too. Okay, then, I'll tell you what happened from my view."

Analysis:

EFFECTIVE. So far, so good.

DIALOGUE #8

Mark:

"Well, at first, I was so excited about my first visit with your group, and when I got home I told my wife all about it and how much I looked forward to going back sometime in the next few months. Then I waited and waited...and waited. You never called. I finally decided that you had changed your mind and didn't want me back.

"That hurt my feelings. Then, when I heard that you were telling people I'm a liar, I got really angry. You should have called, you shouldn't have told people I'd be coming in August without checking the details with me, and you shouldn't have been calling me names. I mean, seriously."

Analysis:

NOT EFFECTIVE. At this point, Mark is taking the whole resolution backward. He is using an accusing tone, instead of speaking in loving terms. He needs to emphasize how he *felt*, not what the other party should have done. This can be accomplished with just a slight change of tone and words. He can say almost exactly the same thing with a minor refocus on being loving. Let's try it again:

DIALOGUE #9

Mark:

"Well, at first, I was so excited about my first visit with your group, and when I got home I told my wife all about it and how much I looked forward to going back sometime in the next few months. Then I waited for your call. When I didn't hear from you, I started worrying that you had changed your mind and didn't want me back.

"I started feeling hurt, and wondered if I hadn't helped you as much as I thought. I should have called you at that point, instead of letting things fester. But I didn't want to be pushy, so I just waited, hoping you would call and want me to come again.

"Then I heard from someone that you were spreading some negative things about me, and it really hurt my feelings. I felt so bad, because I wanted so much to help you. I just couldn't believe the things people told me you were saying. I kept thinking about how they weren't true, instead of just asking you directly. I should have called you immediately, since in truth I assumed that you didn't really say these things. But I was worried that maybe you did say them, so I didn't call. That was cowardly of me.

"The more I thought about these things that I heard you said, the more hurt and angry I felt. I kept wishing that you had called and set a date for August, and I kept wishing that you wouldn't say negative things about me. I also kept wishing that you had called when you heard other people saying these things.

"I guess I kept thinking that you should fix everything, instead of taking responsibility to just call you and find out the truth. Now that I know what really happened, I can see how stupid I was to doubt you. I hope you can forgive me. I could have saved us both a lot of headaches by just calling you, right?"

Analysis:

EFFECTIVE. How would you respond to this if you were Connor? Mark has made it so easy to just forgive him and want the whole thing to be in the past. This is the power of quality, open, loving communication. It heals, soothes, and releases pain. Instead of blaming or subtly lecturing, Mark takes responsibility even as he shares his viewpoint—just as Connor did in the later quotes in the last chapter.

Also, Mark's last sentence expresses what both of these men should have done. Without lecturing, Mark points out what he should have done himself—and it probably won't be lost on Connor that this is exactly true of him as well.

Don't Skip Step 3

It is important to do Step 3 even when Steps 1 and 2 have resolved many of the misunderstandings and hurt feelings. Even if you both feel reconciled after Step 2, the other person needs the positive feelings that come from really knowing what was going on in your mind. And he needs to put his own imaginings about things to rest as well.

So *do* talk through the issues—he needs to hear it from your perspective, and you need to share your views of the conflict, so both of you can avoid letting any residual feelings fester and grow.

Don't Do It!

As the conversation continues, it is very important not to make a common but hurtful mistake. Put simply: Don't assign motives to the other person or speak in attacking ways. For example, say, "You didn't call, and I felt…" but *don't* say "You didn't call *on purpose*, and that *made* me feel…"

Reread these two sentences just to be sure the difference is clear:

- "You didn't call, and I felt…"
- "You didn't call *on purpose*, and that *made* me feel…"

In the first sentence, the speaker just states two facts: (1) you didn't call, and (2) I felt.

In the second sentence, the speaker assigns motives when he says, "You didn't call *on purpose*," and then he assigns blame when he says, "and that *made* me feel..."

Both the assigning of motives and the blame feel accusing and upset, tempting the listener to feel and respond defensively, whereas in the first sentence it just feels like the speaker's view of what happened.

Likewise, share the tough issues without being dogmatic. For example, don't use emotionally charged phrases: "You always...," "You never...," or "You meant to...," etc. Often the best thing to say is "I felt...," since it helps the other person empathize and understand your emotional bank account.

In short, give the other person as many benefits of the doubt as you possibly can. The Bible states: "Love covers a multitude of sins." Share lovingly how you feel, effectively seeking to be understood by focusing on what you experienced, not on what you made up in your mind about why the other person was doing what he did, and not by lecturing him about how he blew it and how he should have acted.

To be understood, share your experience and how it made you feel; don't comment on the other person's thoughts, intentions, or behaviors.

The Pendulum Power of Conflicts

When both parties have openly, clearly, and lovingly shared their perspectives and concerns and both feel heard and understood, a real and full conflict resolution can occur. In fact, this can leave both parties with a *better* relationship and connection than they had before the conflict. But this won't happen unless there is real resolution, and this requires both parties to feel truly understood.

When both feel heard and genuinely understood, a powerful potential future is created. This is a profound moment for everyone involved, because it opens up more possibilities than existed before the two parties met and talked. Just as mistakes can lead to greater growth and leadership if they are handled correctly, conflicts that are positively resolved can set the stage for bigger and better cooperation and teamwork and for profound synergy.

Great leaders know that together Steps 1–3 build the foundation for an incredible amount of increased potential. As the *New York Times* best-selling book *Crucial Conversations* teaches, the key to important communication, especially where negatives are part of the situation, is to find ways to end the "accuse/counter-accuse cycle" and "bring new, helpful information to the table." This is what the first 3 Steps are designed to accomplish. When you do this effectively, either as one of the parties in a conflict or as a leader helping others resolve their concerns, you often create an environment with high potential for serious gains beyond just the conflict resolution.

Just as a pendulum gains energy by swinging higher on one side, hurts and negatives create more potential energy for good when things are truly resolved and passions and relationships swing once more toward shared goals. This can lead to truly exponential leaps of success for all involved. To get there, however, each step must be fully accomplished.

And before you move on to other projects or plans, it is vital to implement Steps 4 and 5. None of the 5 Steps of the process are optional or elective if your goal is true reconciliation and creating the conditions of greater synergy and cooperation.

SUMMARY

Step 3

Once Steps 1 and 2 are complete,
but not earlier, lovingly seek
to be understood.

Share your thoughts and feelings
about the situation in a loving manner.

It is important for you to get
your words and feelings out in the open,
and for the other person to hear them.

If you lean toward
reprimanding rather than loving,
be especially loving.

Make sure the other person is experiencing
your words as loving—your good
intentions aren't enough.

Don't ever justify, blame, or lecture
as you share—this isn't loving.

Focus on how you feel,
not on what the other person
should have done.

Don't assign motives to
the other person.

Don't speak in attacking or
accusing words or tones.

Keep in mind that your goal
is resolution!

Don't be dogmatic or use
emotionally charged words.

Remember that done well,
resolution can make the future
relationship and your shared goals
and projects even stronger.

Don't ever rush on to the next Step,
but take the time to truly do each
Step well! You want this
to work.

STEP 4

Own the Responsibility and Sincerely Apologize

During Steps 1–3, begin taking responsibility for as much of the conflict as possible within the realm of truth. Orrin Woodward said: "Real leaders search for ways to be responsible while protecting the ego of the other party. It takes two to tango, and it takes two to conflict.

"None of us are perfect, so if there is a conflict, you can truthfully take some of the responsibility for it. Even if you were clueless that a conflict was occurring, you can take responsibility for not communicating more clearly and knowing how the other person was feeling."

Of course, it is essential that your words are genuine and honest, but begin taking responsibility as soon as you see anything you could have done better. Most people can see words or actions they might have improved on right from the beginning of any reconciliation. Don't keep these things to yourself; own your responsibility, openly vocalize it, and say you're sorry.

Do this at any point during the resolution or even before you meet. And do it repeatedly. When you know you were wrong about something, with someone who should be a friend, openly take responsibility.

The one caveat is if the situation seems to be headed to a lawsuit, you might want to be careful about what you admit to. But as painful and expensive as lawsuits can be, if you can wisely avoid one by being humble and taking responsibility, do so. By the time you have progressed through Steps 1–3, you should have a clear sense of whether any specific conflict is headed for a real resolution. If so, you may feel more comfortable about opening up.

But in the cases where you are dealing with a friend (or someone who should be a friend) and trying to clear up a misunderstanding or other conflict, be open and genuine, and take full responsibility for everything you can within the realm of truth—as mentioned above. When you do this, you are signaling that you are truly doing your very best, everything you can, to resolve the situation and restore full feelings of fellowship and cooperation. This is powerful.

If You Don't Know, Find Out

Also, know yourself well enough to know if you have any blind spots in being able to see when you are at fault or could take responsibility. Some people struggle with this. They are able to clearly note the faults of others but have a very hard time seeing how they themselves could have done anything better. If you are sure this doesn't apply to you, it probably does!

Humbly ask a mentor or close friend you trust if this is something you need to work on. Knowing this is essential, and the more you need it, the less likely you are to realize it. As Chris Brady ironically put it: "Your self-deception is very annoying to me. I don't have any whatsoever of my own." Funny, but sad when someone really thinks this way.

Ask. If you need to get better at noticing your own mistakes or areas where you should take responsibility, you'll need to practice and improve on this skill before you find yourself in a conflict or trying to resolve a conflict. Think of it from the perspective of the other people in your life: There are few undertakings as difficult as working with people who think they are always right and that everyone else is to blame for any conflicts that arise.

If you think this could describe you, find out. If you are sure it never describes you, find out immediately! Read the excellent book *Dealing with Difficult People* by the Life Leadership Essentials Series, and pay close attention to the types of difficult people it discusses. Again, ask a mentor or close friend if you sometimes fall into any of the types outlined in the book. Ask someone you can really trust to tell you straight, and then be humble about trying to change if they tell you it is needed.

Owning Responsibility is Healing

When you own responsibility for things, it is very healing. When you don't, it can really hurt. As Woodward put it: "Humans have a seemingly limitless ability to deceive themselves. Self-deception allows you to place all the blame, all the responsibility, and all the need for apologies to the other party! This leaves you with all the hurt.

"In order to combat self-deception, pause before you judge. Pray before you become bitter. Think about the entire situation from the vantage point of the other participant. Maybe he or she is clueless that there is even a problem. Maybe you did play a part in the misunderstanding. Empathy is the ability to view the situation from the other person's perspective, and it is essential in combatting self-deception.

"Empathy frees you and allows you to let go of the offense by understanding the conflict from the other side of the table. This helps you replace a judgmental spirit with a grateful, forgiving spirit. Think through the chain of events, asking yourself, 'What could I have done differently?' By making each conflict a teachable moment, one learns many lessons to apply in the future.

"The bigger the leader, the quicker he is to take responsibility and seek resolution…the leader always apologizes first and focuses on the other person's positions, addressing the issue but not attacking the person. Remember, *hurting* people hurt. So conflict *will* happen. But instead of having a judging spirit, do your best to have a spirit of grace."

Responsibility = Trust

If you don't take responsibility for everything you could have done better, you'll be bad at resolving conflicts, and many people won't want to work with you. This is a sure way to weaken your influence and undermine your potential leadership and success.

As Judith Glaser put it in her outstanding book *Conversational Intelligence,* "When we lose our trust, we lose our voice." This is very real. Glaser continued: "Conversations are not what we think they are. We've grown up with a narrow view of conversations, thinking they are about talking, sharing information, telling people what to do, or telling others what's on our minds. We are now learning, through neurological and cognitive research, that a 'conversation' goes deeper and is more robust than simple information sharing...."

"Conversational Intelligence is what separates those who are successful from those who are not—in business, in relationships, and even in marriage." She goes on to show that conversations aren't just our main method of communication, but also our chief mode of connection. When we get our conversations wrong, we often hurt our relationships. This supports what Covey taught about "the emotional bank account."

When it is time to take responsibility, we reach a natural turning point in any conflict resolution. Every chance we miss to take honest responsibility when we should or could is a strike against us. It shows our immaturity and exposes our weaknesses. Strong people open themselves to the vulnerability of vocally taking responsibility and apologizing.

This is an indispensable part of leadership. Without it, no leadership exists, because trust is broken. Leaders take responsibility—not just for any mistakes but also for not stepping up and doing anything they could have done to avoid problems or make things better.

A big person owns this and says so. This is a larger issue than just "Everything I Need to Know I Learned in Kindergarten." It is also a *physical* reality in relationships. Glaser wrote: "Every conversation we have with another person has a chemical component. Conversations have the power to change the brain—they stimulate the production of hormones and neurotransmitters, stimulate body systems and nerve pathways, and change our body's chemistry..."

When we are in the midst of a tense communication, one where the stakes are high and the emotions are vulnerable, like any attempt at conflict resolution, the chemical impact of a conversation can, in Glaser's words, change our brain chemistry "...not just for a moment but perhaps for a lifetime."

Glaser said, "In working with hundreds of companies and tens of thousands of employees in many of the nation's largest organizations over the last thirty years, I've discovered that a lack of Conversational Intelligence (CI) is at the root of many breakdowns in relationships." This is definitely true when there are conflicts between people, and one of the most important areas of Conversational Intelligence is good conflict resolution.

Increase Trust

When we want to be better leaders or to resolve any conflict, we must have real trust. As Glaser pointed out, when trust is absent, we increase conflicts because "we see REALITY through threatened eyes, and we: Reveal less than what we know or what is helpful to move forward, Expect more than what is possible, Assume the worst of others, Look at situations with caution, Interpret communications with fear, Tell secrets we promised not to tell," and say "*Yes* [to] people to avoid confronting truth."

All of these are poor examples of leadership, and they usually cause or heighten conflicts between people. This is why Step 4 is so incredibly important. Only when both parties see and voluntarily accept responsibility for anything they did poorly or could have done better is real trust restored.

When Connor sees Mark taking responsibility, for example, he is willing to accept his apology. Not just consciously, but deep down at the cellular level as well. The same is true when Mark sees Connor taking responsibility. This creates the thoughts and also the feelings of trust. It spreads the chemicals associated with trust through the bodies of both parties. This is why people sometimes shed tears or let out a big sigh of relief in such situations—the physiological responses to conflict and resolution are very real.

Without taking responsibility and apologizing, people can't get to true reconciliation and make it last. Like the bonding a baby feels when it snuggles with its parents, friends trying to overcome a conflict need the reality of genuine trust—and this requires an open, voluntary sharing of responsibility followed by a heartfelt apology from both parties.

When this occurs, it can be very powerful. If it doesn't happen, resolution is lacking. Feelings will remain buried—at least a few of them, however small—and problems will eventually resurface.

Sincerely Apologize

When you take responsibility, sincerely apologize. Do this as many times as it feels appropriate. But always apologize *after* taking responsibility, not absent of it. This turns an apology into a neurological, neurochemical event. In other words, it really works.

As Woodward said: "Apologize from the heart, not just the lips. Really mean it. Such an apology is so powerful and healing. It can truly strengthen relationships, not just resolve a specific conflict. A genuine apology creates more good will than a thousand justifications.

"The higher one climbs on the leadership ladder," he continued, "the more one needs to apologize—simply because leaders are juggling many things at the same time and inevitably something falls through the cracks.

"Leaders must also learn to *accept* apologies from others, truly harboring no ill feelings. Alexander Pope famously taught that to err is human, to forgive is divine. Leaders will err, leading to apologies; leaders will be apologized to, leading to forgiving."

In nearly all cases, if the other party has been truly affirmed (Step 1); has been listened to until he knows he has actually been understood (Step 2); has learned the truth about your actions, reasons, and intentions instead of trying to figure them out in his imagination (Step 3); has felt your love and genuine concern for him (throughout Steps 1–4); and has received the apology of someone who took truthful responsibility for at least part of what happened (Step 4), that party's willingness to accept some responsibility for the conflict is increased, making mutual resolution possible.

Control Your Thoughts

Once you have taken responsibility for your part in the events and apologized for them, and once the other person has done the same, don't allow stinkin' thinkin' to keep reminding you of everything the other party has done wrong. Move on. He's apologized and you forgave him, so don't let your mind wander back into negative thoughts about him.

And don't allow yourself to think up additional problems that neither of you thought to bring up during the conversation. Remember how you felt and your thoughts of reconciliation when you both took responsibility and apologized. Don't rehash things mentally or give in to the temptation to dredge up more concerns. Once you've connected, maintain the integrity of your thoughts, and don't let them run wild or entertain negatives.

Put it behind you. It's water under the bridge. Be consistent and disciplined in this. Otherwise, you'll just train yourself to be a habitually negative person. Once the two parties have owned their responsibility and apologized, shake hands, and move on. Mean it, and stick with it. Use your full integrity on this.

In short, control your thoughts. Have a go-to plan, some project that you are excited about and working hard on, and whenever your mind tries to dredge up something that's been resolved or think negative things about someone you've reconciled with, train it to immediately refocus on your big plan, and put your energy there — on something that is important and positive, something that demands your best efforts.

Leaders focus on what is really important, not on past issues that have already been resolved. If you want to be a leader, hold yourself perfectly to this standard. This is what top leaders do; otherwise they wouldn't be top leaders.

SUMMARY

Step 4

Take responsibility for as much
of the conflict as possible within
the realm of truth.

It takes two to tango, and none of us
are perfect, so if there is a conflict,
you can truthfully take some of
the responsibility for it.

Even if you were clueless that a conflict was occurring, you can take responsibility for not communicating more clearly and knowing how the other
person was feeling.

Take responsibility,
and then sincerely apologize.

Do this repeatedly, whenever
it is appropriate.

Taking responsibility will not just
help the other person but will also

help you feel better.

Every chance we miss to
take honest responsibility when we should
or could is a strike against us.

Leaders take responsibility — not just for any
mistakes but also for not stepping up and doing
anything they could have done to avoid
problems or make things better.

Leaders don't just sincerely apologize;
they also sincerely accept apologies.

Once you have accepted an apology, move on.
Control your thoughts, and don't rehash old news
or dredge up further negative notions about the
other person. Be disciplined on this.

STEP 5

Seek Agreement

At this point, both sides have affirmed the importance of the relationship, both have been heard, and both have apologized. Both have hopefully felt the power of genuine reconciliation.

Now both parties should seek to improve and strengthen their relationship for the future. This is an essential step, because nothing ever just stays in place. Things change. They either get better or worse, but they are in a constant state of change.

In other words, if the two parties come together and experience a true resolution but then go home and don't positively feed the relationships, things may start moving back in the direction of additional conflict. The Second Law of Thermodynamics applies to relationships — if they aren't improving, they won't just remain static; they'll backtrack.

When you go to the effort of real resolution, you don't want to repeat the problems in the future. To keep things moving in a positive direction, take responsibility to nurture and build the relationship.

It is essential at this point to agree on how to operate more efficiently in the future. Agree that you won't listen to rumors and that you'll call or meet and talk directly. This creates powerful shorthand that can help keep your relationships very strong. Agree that you'll give each other the benefit of the doubt and that if any questions arise, you'll immediately talk to each other. No waiting, no wondering, no doubting. Agree that you'll just talk— every time. This creates a powerful operating basis for lasting friendship and positive relationships.

It basically helps you do all 5 Steps in just the few seconds it takes to dial and talk.

This is critical, because it keeps you from having to repeat episodes of conflict over and over with the same person. If one conflict has arisen, work through the 5 Steps and then agree that you won't repeat the same mistakes in the future. Agree that next time, instead of assuming motives, you'll both just approach each other immediately and directly.

Use the Energy for Positives!

But there is another reason to seek agreement, beyond merely managing things so you don't repeat negative patterns. As we mentioned earlier in this book, when people come together in a genuine reconciliation, it creates a lot of positive energy that can be harnessed and used for many good purposes.

Once the issues and the hurts have been flushed, both parties feel a bond and a rededication to what brought them together in the first place. It is important to cement this connection by immediately discussing how their increased unity can help them and the whole team realize even greater accomplishments.

Never end a conflict resolution without this Step. Always spend some time and energy talking about the future. This is vitally important. It will make the conflict resolution deeper and more lasting, and it can lead to increased success for both parties.

As Woodward put it: "While conflict is a given in human relationships, resolution is a choice: the choice to heal and then do even bigger and better things together." This is so true!

This principle is taught in a number of ways, including the idea that we should learn the Lemon Rule: "When life gives you lemons, make lemonade!" When challenges or difficulties come, use them to make relations and team-work even better than before. This applies to conflict reso-lution as well.

When a conflict occurs, resolve it using the first 4 Steps. Then have the wisdom to also apply Step 5 and make something great out of it. It's not enough to affirm each other, really listen, and then take responsibility and apolo-gize. That's a good start, but without Step 5 it just gets you back to where you were before the conflict.

Don't settle for merely fixing things; make them signifi-cantly better! Seek Agreement on something beyond the conflict that is important and can be great.

Embrace Greatness

That's the leadership approach. Agreeing that your purpose together is much more important than the conflict heals and binds. It makes better partners, friends, colleagues, and leaders out of former adversaries—even if the conflict was mild. And working together to turn the conflict into something great is incredibly powerful.

This was discussed in the Dale Carnegie Training book *Make Yourself Unforgettable*: "The late W. Clement Stone, who created a billion-dollar empire in the insurance business, had a unique way of reacting to bad news. As a matter of personal discipline, he trained himself to exclaim, 'Excellent!' no matter how dire the information might seem. Stone was determined to find the positive opportunity hidden in every disaster. If there was no hidden opportunity, he would create one."

As part of every conflict resolution—whether between you and another person or with you serving as a leader helping other parties—ask yourself what the opportunity is in your conflict. Of course, don't do this until you've completed the first 4 Steps. This would throw a wrench into the whole process.

But once Steps 1–4 have been effectively completed, go immediately to Step 5. Find or create a great opportunity for the two (or more) participants in the conflict to work on together in a way that significantly benefits both of them—and others. This is formidable leadership. It is a clear sign of greatness. Turn the conflict resolution into something wonderful that didn't exist beforehand.

The Law of the Wall

This attitude of greatness is infectious. There is an old saying among historians that a *good* leader must do important things, but a *great* leader is only forged by facing overwhelming odds and doing important things anyway. When conflict resolutions are needed, don't just fix them, but also Seek Agreement on ways to turn them into something great.

There is no better time for this than right after you have connected, bonded, and turned negative feelings in the opposite direction. Chris Brady said, "Leaders must remember they become better equipped during their desert experiences." Continuing this theme, Oliver DeMille and Tiffany Earl wrote in *The Student Whisperer*: "Roadblocks, pitfalls, hurdles and challenges can come anywhere along The Path [of life], and there is a proven formula for getting through them. It is called The Law of the Wall....

"Roadblocks can come in many forms, but one thing is certain: They will come. There simply is no progress... without them. No success is ever attained unless you feel a call[,] take action to achieve it, and then run into significant challenges. These challenges are not just standing in the way of your success; they are opportunities.... Keep in mind that whatever forms the roadblock may take, its purpose is to bring you more success.

"This is The Law of the Wall: If you respond to walls and challenges correctly, they will help you progress much better than you would without them." In learning to climb the walls, we become better, stronger, and more able to do great things. If there were no walls, we wouldn't ever need to improve.

The authors continued: "Anyone who has ever considered the development of a child knows this. The child learns to walk by trying, falling, getting up, and doing it over and over until there is a shuffle, a steady walk, and an eventual run." There is no progress or success unless there are walls, and every wall (or challenge in life) is an opportunity for something great. As Chris Brady put it, "Strong sailors are not made on calm seas."

Peak Performance

This is the crux of Step 5: When you have completed Steps 1–4 and the conflict is *resolved*, remember that it isn't really *solved* until you've found the opportunity it affords. This means coming together and Seeking Agreement on something truly important you need or want to accomplish together.

Brainstorm the opportunity, get excited, make a plan, choose assignments—these are indispensable elements in conflict resolution. Step 5 swings all the momentum of the conflict pendulum powerfully in the direction of greatness, with more impetus because of the conflict. Seek Agreement, and come together on something that really matters. Stephen Covey aptly summarized the principles of Step 5 in one word: "Synergize."

If this Step is skipped, a great opportunity has been missed. Leaders know how to turn every lemon, storm, wall, desert, and problem into something that stalwartly fuels their projects and their success. This kind of unwavering passion makes good men and women great, and great men and women even greater.

This is the "extra mile," the intangible leadership edge, the X factor, the *je ne sais quoi*, the sprint at the end of the marathon (even though the runner is far ahead and will win anyway) that separates *good* from *great*. Step 5 is *true resolution*, because it turns conflict into commitment, and adversity into victory. This is the kind of courageous initiative Chris Brady was describing when he said, "No guts, no story!" and also "Life is too short to be little."

Going directly from the 4 Steps of resolving a conflict to the 5th Step of planning how to achieve something great and amazing is a pinnacle of leadership. It is surprising. It is a *non sequitur*. It isn't, in the words of C. S. Lewis, what anyone would expect. It goes beyond…

And that is the point. It is done by people who refuse to stop walking until they reach the summit, and it creates people who are capable of climbing all the way to the top. Step 5 is the creed of climbers, not just campers. Yes, just getting to base camp is hard work, but it isn't enough.

In addition, knowing that you are headed for Step 5 right from the start of any conflict resolution influences your feelings, attitudes, and words all the way through the other 4 Steps. It sets a tone of victory. It tells everyone participating in the conflict resolution what the real stakes are. It expects them to be leaders and incentivizes them to measure up.

In every conflict resolution, always remember where you are headed. Step 5 is about doing more than is needed, because you can. It is this attitude, above everything else, that makes true winners out of regular people.

SUMMARY

Step 5

Once the issues and the hurts have been flushed, both parties feel a bond and a rededication to what brought them together in the first place.

Agree that in the future you'll both avoid repeating the same mistakes by always talking to each other immediately and directly if any issue ever arises — or even seems to be arising.

It is important to cement this connection by immediately discussing how everyone's increased unity can help them achieve even greater accomplishments.

Always spend some time and energy talking about the future.

As part of every conflict resolution — whether between you and another person or with you serving as a leader helping other parties — ask yourself what the opportunity is in your conflict.

Brainstorm ways to capitalize together
on this opportunity.

Leaders don't settle for fixing a conflict,
they look for ways to cooperatively
turn it into a major victory.

"Life is best lived as an adventure."
— Chris Brady

This is the crux of Step 5: When you have completed
Steps 1–4 and the conflict is resolved, remember that
it isn't really solved until you've found the opportunity it afforded. This means coming together and
Seeking Agreement on something truly important
you need or want to accomplish together.

This leadership attitude of going the extra
mile turns regular people into winners!
It is a key component of greatness.

Conclusion

All leaders—all people, in fact—face times and situations where conflict resolution is necessary. As we've already discussed, avoiding such situations or hoping they'll just disappear nearly always causes negative feelings to fester, increase, and spread. Leaders are much more effective when they consistently and lovingly apply the 8 Vital Principles of Conflict Resolution.

Share these principles with your family members, colleagues, and others you live and work with, and make it a point to turn them into habits in your own life. When conflict resolution is needed, knowing and applying these 8 Principles can make all the difference.

Sources

Chris Brady and Orrin Woodward, *Launching a Leadership Revolution*

Chris Brady and Orrin Woodward, *Living Intentionally for Excellence*

Stephen R. Covey, *The 7 Habits of Highly Effective People*

Dale Carnegie Training, *Make Yourself Unforgettable*

Oliver DeMille and Tiffany Earl, *The Student Whisperer*

Judith E. Glaser, *Conversational Intelligence*

Life Leadership Essentials Series, *Dealing With Difficult People*

The New Testament, Matthew 18

Kerry Patterson, Joseph Grenny, Ron McMillan, Al Switzler, *Crucial Conversations*

Orrin Woodward, "Conflict Resolution — Relationships for Life" (Audio)

Recommended Further Reading and Listening

Orrin Woodward, "Conflict Resolution—Relationships for Life" (Audio)

Bill Lewis, "Handling Confrontation" (Audio)

Chris Brady and Orrin Woodward, *Launching a Leadership Revolution*

Judith E. Glaser, *Conversational Intelligence*

Oliver DeMille and Tiffany Earl, *The Student Whisperer*

Life Leadership Essentials Series, *Dealing With Difficult People*

Life Leadership Essentials Series, *Mentoring Matters*

Stuart Scott, *Communication and Conflict Resolution*

Exodus 23, Matthew 18, Luke 17, 1 Corinthians 6, Matthew 5, Luke 6, Titus 3

Other Books in the LIFE Leadership Essentials Series

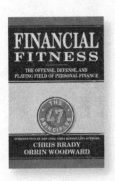

Financial Fitness: The Offense, Defense, and Playing Field of Personal Finance with **Introduction by Chris Brady and Orrin Woodward – $21.95**
If you ever feel that you're too far behind and can't envision a better financial picture, you are so WRONG! You need this book! The *Financial Fitness* book is for everyone at any level of wealth. Just like becoming physically or mentally fit, becoming financially fit requires two things: knowing what to do and taking the necessary action to do it. Learn how to prosper, conserve, and become fiscally fantastic. It's a money thing, and the power to prosper is all yours!

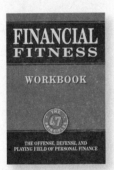

Financial Fitness Workbook **– $7.95**
Economic affairs don't have to be boring or stressful. Make managing money fun in a few simple steps. Use this workbook to get off to a great start and then continue down the right path to becoming fiscally fabulous! Discover exactly where all of your money actually goes as you make note of all your expenditures. Every page will put you one step closer to financial freedom, so purchase the *Financial Fitness Workbook* today and get budgeting!

Mentoring Matters: Targets, Techniques, and Tools for Becoming a Great Mentor with **Foreword by Orrin Woodward – $19.95**
Get your sticky notes ready for all the info you're about to take in from this book. Do you know what it means to be a *great* mentor? It's a key part of successful leadership, but for most people, the necessary skills and techniques don't come naturally. Educate yourself on all of the key targets, techniques, and tools for becoming a magnificent mentor with this easy-to-apply manual. Your leadership success will be forever increased!

Turn the Page: How to Read Like a Top Leader with **Introduction by Chris Brady – $15.95**
Leaders are readers. But there are many ways to read, and leaders read differently than most people do. They read to learn what they need to know, do, or feel, regardless of the author's intent or words. They see past the words and read with the specific intent of finding truth and applying it directly in their own lives. Learn how to read like a top leader so you'll be better able to emulate their success. Applying the skills taught in *Turn the Page* will impact your life, career, and leadership abilities in ways you can't even imagine. So turn the page and start reading!

SPLASH!: A Leader's Guide to Effective Public Speaking with **Foreword by Chris Brady – $15.95**
For many, the fear of giving a speech is worse than the fear of death. But public speaking can be truly enjoyable *and* a powerful tool for making a difference in the lives of others. Whether you are a beginner or a seasoned orator, this book will help you transform your public speaking to a whole new level of leadership influence. Learn the SPLASH formula for great public speaking that will make you the kind of speaker and leader who makes a SPLASH—leaving any audience, big or small, forever changed—every time you speak!

The Serious Power of Fun with **Foreword by Chris Brady – $15.95**
Life got you down? Feeling like life isn't much fun is a bad place to be. Fun matters. It is serious business and a source of significant leadership power. Without it, few people maintain the levels of inspired motivation and sustained effort that bring great success. So put a smile back on your face. Discover how to make every area of life more enjoyable and turn any situation into the right kind of fun. Learn to cultivate a habit of designed gratification—where life just keeps getting better—and *laugh your way to increased success* with *The Serious Power of Fun!*

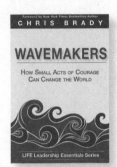

Wavemakers: How Small Acts of Courage Can Change the World **with Foreword by Chris Brady – $15.95**
Every now and then, extraordinary individuals come along who make huge waves and bring about permanent change in the lives of so many that society as a whole is forever altered. Discover from the examples of the various "Wavemakers" showcased in this book how you can make waves of your own and change the world for the better!

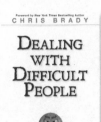

Dealing with Difficult People with Foreword **by Chris Brady – $15.95**
How many times have you felt like banging your head against the wall trying to figure out how to deal with a routinely difficult person, whether at work or in your personal life? You can't control others, but you can control how you handle them. Learn about the seven main types of difficult people and the Five-Step Peace Process, and equip yourself to understand why people behave the way they do, break the cycle of frustration, and turn your interactions into healthy, productive experiences. "You are going to encounter difficult people. Plan on it. Prepare for it. Become good at it."

Thick-Skinned: Why Caring Too Much about What Other People Think and Say Is Holding You Back— And What to Do about It **with foreword by Claude Hamilton- $15.95**
The downfall of many people is in worrying about what others think. Having thick skin is the exact ingredient that can help those who are looking to round out this area of their lives that often holds them back. This book will help you figure out why you are thin-skinned, show you how to ignore the negative speak from others and focus on positive thoughts instead, and teach you ways to develop thicker skin so you can flourish without hesitation.

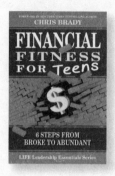

Financial Fitness for Teens with Foreword **by Chris Brady – $15.95**
The downfall of many people is in worrying about what others think, sometimes to the detrimental point of losing their motivation and giving up. Having thick skin is the exact ingredient that can help those who are looking to round out this area of their lives that often holds them back. This book will help you figure out why you are thin-skinned, show you how to ignore the negative speak from others and focus on positive thoughts instead, and teach you ways to develop thicker skin so you can flourish without hesitation.

Subscriptions and Products from LIFE Leadership

Rascal Radio Subscription – $49.95 per month
Rascal Radio by LIFE Leadership is the world's first online personal development radio hot spot. Rascal Radio is centered on LIFE Leadership's 8 Fs: Faith, Family, Finances, Fitness, Following, Freedom, Friends, and Fun. Subscribers have unlimited access to **hundreds and hundreds** of audio recordings that they can stream endlessly from both the **LIFE Leadership website** and the **LIFE Leadership Smartphone App.** Listen to one of the preset stations or customize your own based on speaker or subject. Of course, you can easily skip tracks or "like" as many as you want. And if you are listening from the website, you can purchase any one of these incredible audios.

Let Rascal Radio provide you with **life-changing information to help you live the life you've always wanted!**

The LIFE Series – $50.00 per month
Here's where LIFE Leadership began—with the now famously followed 8 Fs: Family, Finances, Fitness, Faith, Following, Freedom, Friends, and Fun. This highly recommended series offers a strong foundation on which to build and advance in every area of your daily life. The timeless truths and effective strategies included will reignite passion and inspire you to be your very best. Transform your life for the better and watch how it will create positive change in the lives of those around you. Subscribe today and have the time of your LIFE!

Series includes 4 audios and 1 book monthly and is also available in Spanish and French.

The LLR (Launching a Leadership Revolution) Series – $50.00 per month

There is no such thing as a born leader. Based on the *New York Times* bestseller *Launching a Leadership Revolution* by Chris Brady and Orrin Woodward, this series focuses on teaching leadership skills at every level. The principles and specifics taught in the LLR Series will equip you with all the tools you need for business advancement, community influence, church impact, and even an advantage in your home life. Topics include: leadership, finances, public speaking, goal setting,

mentoring, game planning, accountability and tracking of progress, levels of motivation and influence, and leaving a personal legacy. Will you be ready to take the lead when you're called? Subscribe now and learn how to achieve effective confidence skills while growing stronger in your leadership ability.

Series includes 4 audios and 1 leadership book monthly.

The AGO (All Grace Outreach) Series – $25.00 per month

We are all here together to love one another and take care of each other. But sometimes in this hectic world, we lose our way and forget our true purpose. When you subscribe to the AGO Series, you'll gain the valuable support and guidance that every Christian searches for. Nurture your soul, strengthen your faith, and find answers to better understand God's plan for your life, marriage, and children.

Series includes 1 audio and 1 book monthly.

The Edge Series – $10.00 per month

You'll cut in front of the rest of the crowd when you get the *Edge*. Designed for those on the younger side of life, this hard-core, no-frills series promotes self-confidence, drive, and motivation. Get advice, timely information, and true stories of success from interesting talks and fascinating people. Block out the noise around you and learn the principles of self-improvement at an early age. It's a gift that will keep on giving from parent to child. Subscribe today and get a competitive *Edge* on tomorrow.

Series includes 1 audio monthly.

Financial Fitness Subscription – $10.00 per month for 12 months

If you found the *Financial Fitness Pack* life-changing and beneficial to your bank account, then you'll want even more timely information and guidance from the Financial Fitness Subscription. It's designed as a continuing economic education to help people develop financial discipline and overall knowledge of how their money works. Learn how to make financial principles your financial habits. It's a money thing, and it always pays to be cash savvy.

Subscription includes 1 audio monthly.

***Financial Fitness Pack –
$99.99***

Once and for all, it's time to
free yourself from the worry
and heavy burden of debt.
Decide today to take an
honest look at your finances
by learning and applying the
simple principles of financial
success. The *Financial Fitness
Pack* provides you with all
the tools needed to get on
a path to becoming fiscally
fantastic!

Pack includes the Financial
Fitness *book, a companion
workbook, and 8 audio
recordings.*